Little Book of

Prayers

for

New Thought
Christians

Elizabeth C. Dixon

Prayers for New Thought Christians

Elizabeth C. Dixon

Dedicated to the lone soul who emerges from sleep in the dark hours to find solace in the respite of prayer.

With special thanks to,
and appreciation for,
Reverend Betty R. Sikking
&
Reverend C. Thomas Sikking
at whose knees I learned
Christian metaphysics.

Elizabeth C. Dixon

CONTENTS

Preface vi

Introduction..3

Preparatory Meditations.................................7

   Quieting Thoughts 9

   Flow of Breath.......................................11

   Now Release..12

   Place of Peace 13

   Inner Portal 14

   Inner Light..15

   True Essence...17

   Moving Beyond 19

   Know Love..20

   Await in Stillness...................................21

   The Presence...22

   The Silence 23

Affirmative Prayers 24
   Visionary Transformation 28
   Power & Peace in The Presence 36
   Restoration & Wholeness 44
   Supernatural Prosperity & Guidance 50
   Liberation of Forgiveness 58
   Sacred Space for Another 64
   Transitions through Eternity 74
   Incarnation & Ascension 80
   Celebration in Gratitude 84
   Master, Teach Us to Pray 90
Duodenaria Prayer Process 92

   Additional Resources 106
   Suggested Reading 107
   About the Author 110
   An Invitation 111

Elizabeth C. Dixon

Therefore I tell you,
whatever you ask for in prayer,
believe that you have received it,
and it will be yours.
Mark 11:24

Preface

Prayer is considered by some to be elevated thought. Prayer can also be described as one's highest intention. It is sometimes said that prayer is talking to God and meditation is listening to God. Some consider prayer to be a sacred state of being. The common thread of the many and varied concepts of prayer and ways of praying is that it is the human aspiration and activity of accessing a mystical connection with the Most High.

Whatever our belief, our style, our ability, or our concept of God, He/She/It meets us right where we are in our human consciousness and situation. Simply in our intention of holding spiritual space, our consciousness is lifted. By the mere act of praying, we are declaring and affirming that God is accessible and greater than any appearance, circumstance, or condition.

Elizabeth C. Dixon

May the following 12 preparatory meditations, 40 affirmative prayers, including my original interpretive Lord's Prayer, and the culminating Duodenaria Prayer process that comprise this diminutive trove serve to move you into a greater realization of the truth of your being and inspire in you an expanded experience of GOD.

Introduction

God is All, and as spiritual beings, our fundamental and natural essence is already one with God. Separation from God is an illusion we believe due to our limited awareness as humans having a physical experience in a physical universe. We pray in order to reconnect with the Divine Essence of our being and focus on God's infinite goodness within us and within all that is.

Prayer does not change God; prayer changes us. God is perfect and constant—absolute. We pray to experience God. We approach the prayer process with a mien of allowing and waiting. As we pray, we are expanded into greater and greater awareness of the Presence of the Spirit of God moving around, in, and through us and everything. As the experience of God quickens within us, we are healed, guided, prospered, protected, assured, and sustained—*made whole*—by becoming more

3

fully aligned with The One. The experience of God is an ineffable experience of Perfect Love.

For New Thought Christians, our Elder Brother and Wayshower, Jesus Christ, is our model and the example of indwelling Divinity realized and fully expressed in human form. The Christ is that spark of Divinity within each of us as creations and extensions of The Source—God. The resurrected Jesus Christ is the promise of victory over our sense of separation from God—death—and thereby our salvation, in this life and the next. Through prayer, we bring our Christ nature—our connection with God—into conscious awareness.

The New Thought Movement practices affirmative prayer. Affirmative prayer is a positive, life-enhancing approach to prayer. It is not a practice of begging or beseeching God. We do not pray to influence or persuade God to do something. Rather, we pray to expand our awareness of God and align ourselves with Life Force Energy, Source, to become partners in sacred co-creation. Co-creating with God is the mechanism by which our prayers are made manifest, first in our consciousness and then in the out-pictured world.

We address God in our prayers by whatever Name resonates in us at our deepest level of being as the Highest Idea that we are capable of entertaining. Perhaps it is "Creator," "First Cause," or "Source." Perhaps it is more intimate or hierarchical, such as "Father," or "Mother-Father God," or "Lord." Some perceive God in the abstract without reference to entity or being-ness, but rather as Principle, or as a concept or activity, such as "All That Is," "Divine Mind," "I Am," or yes, even as "The Force." Whatever sacred Name one is led to use in prayer is appropriate for that person. The Name you conceive God by will itself feel like a prayer.

Elizabeth C. Dixon

"I Am that I Am . . . ." Exodus 3:14

Preparatory Meditations

The activity of prayer can happen in any place, at any time, and in any circumstance known to the human experience. Certainly, the power and efficacy of prayers when expressed in the midst of chaos and confusion, during extreme pain and duress, and from the depths of despair, have been felt and witnessed by most of us at one time or another. The prayers offered in this book, however, are of a devotional, contemplative nature, intended to inspire and expand consciousness.

Perhaps you will find that a brief period of preparation ahead of your praying will assist you in having the most optimal experience. As you intentionally relax the body and quiet the mind, you will begin to feel an inner shift happening at deep levels—allowing you to have a transformative prayer event. And perhaps as part of this meditative process you will feel moved to simply sit in The Silence and wait—in a receptive, open state—and allow Spirit to convey Its message to you.

Each of the following introspective meditations can usher you into a serene and focused prayerful state. Choose one of these inductions and read it slowly as a precursor to your prayer activity. Rather than simply reading the passages, *experience* them. I invite you to allow the words of these opening meditations to process within you as though they are being expressed in your own inner voice.

But whenever you pray, go into your room
and shut the door and pray to your Father
who is in secret; and your Father
who sees in secret will reward you.
Matthew 6:6

Quieting Thoughts

As I make adjustments to my body position that will contribute to my comfort and relaxation, I breathe into the Now moment. Breathing in . . . and out. Slowly . . . deeply. I begin to notice that as I take deep . . . cleansing breaths . . . slowly, regularly . . . that I am becoming more centered . . . more relaxed . . . easily.

It's as if a gentle wave of relaxation is slowly rolling down through my body, from the top of my head, all the way down through my torso and pelvis . . . through my legs . . . and to the tips of my toes. As I breathe in . . . and out. Relaxation . . . flowing.

A lovely sensation of calm . . . and balance . . . envelops me as I turn within. Any distracting thought that comes up, I notice, and then I just allow it to fade away . . . fade away like a wisp of smoke disappearing on a gentle breeze. It fades away like a snowflake melting on the warm palm of my hand.

And if a thought begins to intrude, I can just let it diminish into nothingness . . . like the mist over a pond that vanishes in the morning sunshine. How comforting the quiet. How soothing the *stillness*.

Flow of Breath

As I prepare for prayer, I notice the rhythmic flow of my breathing. So soft and gentle, so easy that it almost begins to feel as if each breath in . . . naturally leads to the next breath out. And that breath out . . . easily leads to the next breath in. Each breath in . . . naturally leads to the next breath out . . . that leads to the next breath in. I begin to feel as if my breath is becoming a circle of breath.

As each breath in . . . leads gently to the next breath out . . . that leads to the next breath in, I notice how naturally that is happening . . . beginning to feel as if the breath is a continuous, relaxing circle of breath. A circle of breath, as if it has a flow of energy all its own. Easy, gentle, peaceful, continuous circle of breath. Flowing, I begin to notice myself inside of this energy . . . inside this circle of life-sustaining breath. A flowing circle. Life, *breathing*, in me.

Now Release

Breathing in . . . and out . . . I notice that this Now present moment is where I live and move and have my being. In this Now moment, all fears . . . all anxieties just dissolve away, because those thoughts are about the past . . . or the future . . . and I am in the Now moment, calm, relaxed, intentionally releasing those thoughts.

I am willing to let go of anything and everything that does not serve me in this Now moment. I open my hands in a gesture of release and breathe in . . . and out. I am willing to let go of expectation, let go of judgment, let go of thought . . . and just be. I am willing to release all concerns and burdens to God, now. I let go. *I let God.*

Place of Peace

With my hands lying open and my jaw loose and relaxed, I enjoy the sensation of taking several deep, slow, cleansing breaths. I feel the air fill my body temple . . . all the way down into my abdomen . . . all the way back into my spine. If I notice an area of tension or discomfort somewhere, I just breathe comfort into that spot now and watch as it relaxes and loosens.

That's right . . . every breath spreads through me . . . comforting and soothing whatever might need attention in the body . . . as it flows, easily. And I find that I naturally turn my focus within. Going inward . . . to that place of safety and familiarity . . . deep inside me. Always present . . . within . . . constant.

This is my place of peace. So still . . . so quiet. Here, I am fully supported. Here is where my true essence abides . . . timeless . . . tranquil. This place within, ever available . . . enduring. How lovely . . . the *peace*.

13

Inner Portal

As I breathe in . . . and out . . . slowly . . . deeply . . . my body temple relaxes into lovely comfort . . . naturally. I take a moment to enjoy with wonder all the sensations of *being*.

Now I follow my attention as it moves to the heart space area . . . deep into the core of me. In this inner sanctuary I am safe . . . supported. I dwell here in peace and in anticipation of Good.

Here is the place where I am free to be willing. Here I am willing to surrender to beneficial life force energy. I allow a portal to open within my sanctuary of self. I watch with joy as a sacred portal to The Most High opens.

I am open to receive.

Inner Light

As I find the body position that is just right for me to feel comfortable and calm, perhaps I slowly turn my head to the left, and to the right, slowly stretching my neck. And it might even feel good to roll my shoulders and stretch any extremity that feels it would like to give up some tension.

Now I breathe into the present moment . . . allowing my breathing to flow naturally and calmly. Breathing in . . . *pausing* . . . and breathing out. As my breathing shifts my body . . . into greater comfort and balance . . . I allow my focus to move down into the center of the body. . . to a place deep inside me, perhaps behind and below the breastbone. *Within me.*

I can begin to imagine that a pinpoint of bright white light is appearing there . . . in the depth of my being. There it is . . . like a pinprick in the fabric of eternity . . . opening . . . letting in the light. Clear brightness.

I notice that the light is . . . expanding . . . brighter . . . *within me.* And as it grows . . . warm, gentle energy is filling me. I relax into this expanding light energy as it soothes and balances whatever it touches. So welcomed . . . I glory in it . . . and allow it to fill my whole being. *I am* light.

True Essence

I welcome this time apart and become more aware of my breathing. As I breathe deep, cleansing breaths . . . I begin to notice relaxation spreading through my body. I begin to notice my mind is calming . . . and clearing.

Turning within, now, my focus naturally drops into my heart center. Within me there is a Knowing . . . in the core of my being.

In this place of Knowing, my peace and assurance grow . . . as I sense the presence of Spirit. My awareness of the presence of God now expands.

Here I encounter Truth. Here I begin to realize my true essence is Spirit. My true essence is Spirit. *I Am* free, a spiritual being, unhampered by the limitations of the world. In Spirit *I Am* free. Beyond outer appearances. Beyond temporary conditions. *I Am* Spirit . . . one with God.

Elizabeth C. Dixon

I *Am* a concept in the Mind of God . . . an expression of God Energy . . . and extension of God. I *Am* free. Ever expanding, more and more aware of the truth of my being . . . in the Presense of God within . . . in the inner Sanctuary . . . I know my true essence is Spirit. *I Am.*

Moving Beyond

Breathing in . . . and out . . . slowly . . . deeply .
. . I am soothed and become naturally centered
and balanced. And as I lean into comfort, my
inner vision is training upward . . . and out,
perhaps as if through the forehead. Out
beyond . . . any confines. My mind feels lighter
. . . freer . . . *expansive*.

I enjoy the wonder of this feeling of ascending.
. . outward . . . to a place of expanded
awareness. Moving into a sense of clarity. . .
and insight. Like floating up . . . a lightness of
mind. Higher and higher . . . insight . . .
expanding, into the Knowing. A greater sense
of access to *All That Is*.

Know Love

As I find a relaxed position, I enjoy several deep breaths and move my focus within. The more often I take a sacred time apart for myself, the more naturally and easily the mantel of peace and comfort settles over me. As I turn inward to that place of familiarity and serenity . . . in my core . . . always present . . . within . . . constant . . .I contemplate Love.

It is Love that sustains me. Love is my Source. The apprehension of God in my human experience is Love. When I experience Love, I feel expanded, energetically and mystically. Beyond words . . . beyond thoughts. Love . . . opens me to receive . . . and to know . . . more of God . . . more of Love. When I experience love, I experience God . . . in Oneness. Love in me is God, expressing in me . . . through me . . . as me. I know Love. I Am Love . . . *I Am Love*, now .

Await in Stillness

Settling into a comfortable position, I enjoy several purposeful breaths that signal my body to relax and my mind to slow down. As I scan my body . . . I notice any place that might be holding some tension . . . and I breathe comfort into that place. Welcoming serenity, I allow any distracting thought that may enter my mind to just fade away, like an echo in a distant canyon, vanishing into nothingness.

I am like a deep, still mountain lake. The surface is a mirror that reflects the sky above. I await in tranquility for the breath of God to move upon me.

Elizabeth C. Dixon

The Presence

As I set my intention to create sacred space within, my breathing is deep and regular. I am not alone—I sense a Presence. Spirit is here, now. With each beat of my heart, my awareness of the Presence of Spirit expands. This is True.

I am connected at all times with the Source of all that *is*. The Life Force that lives and moves and has its being in and through me is one and the same as Infinite Mind—the consciousness of creative intent and the energy of unconditional love. Life is the consciousness of God . . . I now expand in the Presence . . . that *is* God.

"Be still and know that I am God . . . ."
Psalm 46:10

The Silence

As I close my eyes, I breathe into the Now present moment. All around me is stillness . . . all around me is safety. Gently turning within, my knowing grows that this inner sanctuary is my place of peace . . . my place of pure being, ... my place to encounter the timeless and complete Divine. In this silent sanctuary, my awareness of the presence of God expands.

In the presence of The Great I Am, I concede my temporary human condition and release my human need. God is always enough. I am at ease, knowing that God is always present . . . always enough.

Here I begin to realize my core essence truly is spirit. I am ever expanding, more and more aware of the truth of my being . . . God reveals Himself in the Silence . . . in the eternal present moment . . . in the Silence, within . . . in the inner Sanctuary . . . in the Silence . . . in the Silence . . . in the Silence

Affirmative Prayers

*Do not be conformed to this world, but be
transformed by the renewal of your mind, that
you may discern what is the will of God—what
is good and acceptable and perfect.*
Romans 12:2

In New Thought, there is a central tenet that *thought* is the mechanism by which we create, perceive, and experience. Because thinking is generative, every thought is a "prayer," for good or for ill. Merely transitory thoughts that flit through our minds and vanish are innocuous. Intentional thoughts that we nurture and embrace and dwell upon, however, activate the process of manifestation.

Indeed, through the power of thought, especially when combined and reinforced with our emotion and devotion, we become co-creators with God. If our thoughts and feelings are not in alignment with God, Love, we create error and suffering for ourselves and others.

In some quarters of New Thought, worry is considered negative prayer.

Another core concept is that we cannot hold (believe) equally two opposite thoughts in our minds simultaneously; one will dominate. Therefore, whenever we find that we are suffering—from pain, fear, discord, lack, dis-ease, confusion, despair, or any other affliction of mind, body, or soul—positive prayer is the immediate and ready means of relief always available to us. As we allow our awareness of the Presence of God to expand, we *change our thoughts*. As we experience God in prayer, we are transformed—the All Good flows in and through us and manifests Itself in us and in our lives.

How is it that we are able to impact others and the world at large by way of our prayers? In Christ Consciousness we are all connected; therefore, as any one of us expands his or her experience and apprehension of God's Perfect Love, everyone else, and particularly someone who is the focus of our prayers, is also lifted up and supported. Those we pray with and for are moved and spiritually enlivened at deep soul levels by our sacred intent and then have an enriched opportunity for transformation, insofar as their own consciousness is ready.

Come apart from the world for a while now by going within to your inner sanctuary and intentionally entering into the Presence of the Most High for the sacred activity of prayer. Spend several moments in a silent, meditative state, perhaps first reading one of the 12 Preparatory Meditations offered earlier in this book. Slow and deepen the breath and allow your focus to drop into the heart space. Wait in receptivity and allow Spirit to move in and through you. Welcome the coming communion, revelation, and transformation, and *Be Blessed.*

Finally, brethren, whatsoever things are true, whatsoever things are honest, whatsoever things are just, whatsoever things are pure, whatsoever things are lovely, whatsoever things are of good report; if there be any virtue, and if there be any praise, think on these things.
Philippians 4:8

I

Visionary Transformation

Today

Today I rise in expectation to meet my Good.

May I step out confidently, eager to engage in the adventure of living.

May I seek and discover the many wonders and beauty surrounding me.

May I countenance everyone I meet with amity and generosity.

May my words resound with clarity, truth, and compassion.

May my activities contribute positively to the Whole and bring me fulfillment.

Today I walk in the Spirit of Grace, and I am blessed and a blessing! Amen.

I Am Free

As your beloved creation, I am a spiritual Being, unrestrained by the limitations of the world.

I release the chains of the past and invite the possibilities of the future.

In Your Presence I know that to be free means I no longer stand in a place of pain, lack, misery, or fear.

I move forward with the Holy Spirit into healing, prosperity, forgiveness, peace, and joy.

In the freedom of Spirit, I now stand in the fullness of my true nature.

Thank you, God—I am free! Amen.

Divine Synchronicity

Beyond time and structure, You order all things into elegant Harmony, O God.

Every process and activity and event in Your Creation is moved upon by Your Hand.

What a delight to behold the Power of Your perfect Timing in manifestation!

I willingly align with and in You. It is natural and right—I am also Your Creation, beloved. From this accord come my Blessings.

Your Purposes ultimately prevail in the world and in my life in wondrous synchronicity.

I stand amazed! Thank You, God!

Highest Good

O Lord, I welcome the peace that comes with the certainty that Your Grace and Power transcend all understanding and all appearances.

May I experience Your all-providing Love moving through my body, mind, affairs, and concerns as I recognize Your Activity in things both great and minute.

Instead of looking for evidence of what is "wrong" in the world, may I open my spiritual eyes to see Truth and Beauty expressing all around me.

May I know that beyond my current limited human vision, You are indeed at work and in charge, and all is well in my life and in the lives of my loved ones as Your Plan for our Highest Good unfolds.

You have promised us the Kingdom! Thank You, God! Amen.

Transformation

Wrapped in Your Love and Light, God, I now entrust my deepest needs to You.

I willingly surrender my concerns to you in hope and faith.

In You alone do I find my sweet release and blessed relief.

My burdens relinquished to You, I have now cleared an open space within me to receive Your Blessings.

Vibrant health, abundant prosperity, inspired ideas, harmonious relationships, joyful well-being, and Divine order prevail in all my affairs.

Expectancy fills my being, and I am eager to engage in what is mine to do with renewed vigor and enthusiasm.

As my awareness and experience of You expands, I begin to realize that the abundant Life is indeed an ever-expanding consciousness of You, God, and All that You Are.

As I empty of self, the Christ Light moves in and through me, as me, and I am transformed!

Thank you, Creator God, Source of All! Amen.

I Co-Create

Thoughts are generative, therefore I am always one sustained thought away from a new and different life.

You have given me dominion over my thoughts, so I always have the freedom and power to choose what they will be. Such is the dynamic partnership You have established with us, O God!

Let me remember that where attention goes, creative energy flows. My thoughts activate expansion and attraction in the vast field of potentiality that is God Substance, and my life experience is thereby wondrously created.

Giving my attention to the good in my life allows it to increase. As I choose to fix my focus on the beautiful and the peaceful, I find myself dwelling in beauty and peace.

As I contemplate and activate wholesome and harmonious pursuits, I naturally live a healthy life of well-being and harmony.

If ever I am tempted by diminishing and destructive thoughts, I know I can immediately re-center my mind in You, God. Recognizing and experiencing Your Presence instantly returns my thoughts to clarity and creativity.

Gently whisper to me the reminder that You have given me the honor of sacred agency with You as a co-creator, through the power of my chosen thoughts and words and activities.

May I be ever mindful of my charge to think and speak in alignment with You!

Let the musings and ponderings of my mind and soul be expressions of celebration and praise of Holy Mind!

Thank You, Living, Loving, Creating God! Amen.

II

Power & Peace in The Presence

Parousia

Come Spirit, come! You know my heart; You draw me close to You. You have assured us that even before we ask, You are already answering. Be with me now, I pray.

I simply wait in receptivity as the Light of Your Perfect Love shines upon me, and gently I become aware that You are here.

May my intuition and experience of Your continual Countenance grow. May I realize evermore that Your perpetual Presence is sustaining me, uplifting me, and guiding me—always available, constant.

Expand my awareness of Your Presence, both now in this Sacred moment and as I advance into each day and night to come. Where I am, You Are! Amen.

Proceed in the Presence

I walk with You each day, God. You are my strength and security along my way. You are the Light upon my path, the Guide within my soul, and the Order in my steps.

If ever I face a difficult situation, I lean into you, God, in faith that Your Power will sustain me through it or lift me above it and set me aright to continue toward my Good.

Aligned in the flow of Your Perfect Love, I am carried forward and upward into greater and greater consciousness and experience of You.

In Your Presence I proceed in Peace.

By the Power of the Christ indwelling, it is so! Amen.

Elizabeth C. Dixon

Omnipotence Protects Me

I breathe into the now present moment as I become still and know: God, Your all-powerful, protecting Presence surrounds me, and all is well.

You are a certain, unassailable citadel in every situation, bringing calm and stability to my mind, body, and activities.

I keep my focus trained on you, God. In Your Presence I am filled with assurance, strength, and courage. Your Light surrounds me, and I know what to do.

I thank you for Your all-encompassing, loving Power that is now moving in and through me and in the midst of my circumstances, making the way ahead safe and tractable.

Your Perfect Love lifts me above and beyond all temporal conditions. I am thrilled with gratitude. Thank you, God! In the name of the Christ, it is so! Amen!

Periphery

Lord, out on the periphery there is activity and strife and noise.

A cacophony of effort and concern
and involvement and participation
and demand and requirement
surrounds me, out there, on the periphery.

Out there, a billion stories are in the process of unfolding. You are simultaneously there in the midst of them all and in charge, both known and unknown.

My attention is not required on the periphery. It is not mine to manage—God is there, being God.

I now withdraw my focus and concern from the circumference and retreat to my center. God is here . . . in the stillness . . . at my core.

I am serene. Amen.

My Assurance

I am always secure in Your care, O God!

In Your keeping I live each day, each moment, with refreshed strength and peace, enjoying an ever-renewing sense of purpose and joy in living.

In Your guiding, protecting Light, I walk with poise and confidence. You are always present, assuring me that all things are working together for my Highest Good, and all is well.

Your Love is constantly moving through me, renewing my body temple as every living cell responds to Your energizing, sustaining Power.

The continuous flow of Your all-providing Substance manifests as order, prosperity and blessings in my life circumstances. I remain open to receive, trusting You.

You are mightily at work in my life, in the lives of my loved ones, and in the whole world, even beyond our present limited perceptions and understanding.

I affirm and declare these Truths in gratitude and thanksgiving.

By the Power and in the Name of Christ indwelling, assurance is mine! Amen.

Enlarge My Vision

O God, in this world we have trouble! As I survey the world, too often I witness adversity, violence, and misery, and I feel dismayed and distraught.

My heart grieves over the loss and suffering borne by so many. Troubles so hard, only You know!

As I behold the fallen state of the world, overwhelm and discouragement creep in to tempt me with despair.

Leave me not in temptation, O Lord! Let me take courage and refuge in You Who have overcome the world!

You assure us that struggle and sorrow are our temporary, mortal responses and perceptions to a temporal and imperfect physical existence.

We are spiritual beings—not bound by the physical! Lift me up above and beyond my limited human vision, I pray!

In You there is no loss; Your Perfect Love transcends the world and restores all things to Wholeness in Spirit.

Only in You do I find real and lasting peace. I keep my focus singly upon You and I am expanded beyond the world! Amen!

III

Restoration & Wholeness

I Am Whole

As Your creation, God, my natural state is Wholeness. Health is my normal condition.

Your creative, dynamic Energy enlivens and strengthens every fiber of my being, constantly renewing me at the cellular level.

Your Love pulses through my body temple, invigorating and sustaining it continually.

I am one with the One. In You I enjoy effulgent health and well-being. I am whole, as You created me to be.

There is nothing to be healed; only the Truth to be revealed.

You are filling me now and evermore with Your Perfect Life. Thank You, God! Amen.

Divine Life Energy

How wondrously You have made me, O God! I thrill with the knowing that my very existence is an expression of Your Divine Life Energy.

It is only in You that I live and move and breathe and have being.

As Your life-sustaining Love and Light actuate through me, I radiate strength, vitality, and health as I proceed through my days.

In Your Presence I remember the Truth of my Being, and I am restored!

In the Name and by the Power of the Indwelling Christ, I declare it to be so! Amen.

Gather Me Up

Lord, I have scattered my energy and attention far and wide into many disparate places and pursuits. Send now the Holy Spirit to gather up my fractured parts, I pray, and center all of me once again in You.

As I train my focus on You, God, Divine Order is established and all that concerns and affects me is set into a beneficial and dynamic process for my unification.

By returning my awareness to You, God, I am healed and renewed. Aligned in Your Perfect Love I experience power and peace. In You I am whole.

Christ in me is One with All That Is.
We are Integral! Praise God!

*Do you not know that you are God's temple
and that God's Spirit dwells in you?*
I Corinthians 3:16

Elizabeth C. Dixon

Spiritual Treatment

I exist within the Whole that Is God.
The Wholeness of All that Is, is accessible
within me.
As a drop in the ocean that is also the ocean, I
am one with All that God Is, inseparable.
God's all-powerful Presence suffuses my
essence.
My body is the temple of the Living God.
There is latent within me the perfect pattern of
the Christ Body.
As I realize that I am one with the One, I
become attuned and aligned with It.
I am an individualized energetic expression of
God, the One.
I am expanding in Consciousness.
I am growing in Perfect Love.
I am transcending temporal conditions.
I now know the Truth of my Being.
Vitality is now emerging.
Healing is now spreading.
Harmony is now resounding.
Ideas are now birthing.
Channels of prosperity are now opening.

Divine Order is now establishing.
My heart is swelling in gratitude and joy as I receive the Good that is continuously flowing to and through me.
In Christ Consciousness I am transformed!
Thank you, God, it is so! Amen.

This Spiritual Treatment can be administered to another by substitution of the word "you" for "I." It can be applied in person or remotely.

The laying-on of hands by gentle touch or near touch can assist in heightening the efficacy. When remotely administering the Treatment, see the recipient in your mind's eye. The subject will benefit whether s/he has been informed of your praying or not; even unconscious people are affected by Spiritual Treatment.

As your Consciousness lifts and expands, the person with and for whom you are praying is also lifted and expanded in Consciousness.

Love and belief are the operative agents. Healing begins in Spirit and manifests in the physical. And so it is!

IV

Supernatural Prosperity & Guidance

True Prosperity

Living, Loving, Creating God, You are Source; You are All Sufficiency!

As Your beloved creation, I rely on Your provision to fulfill my every good desire.

You have promised that it is Your good pleasure to give us the Kingdom, and so I now release my human need to you and affirm that any idea of lack is but an illusion.

As I align with You with a thankful heart, I open myself to receive Your always-flowing abundant Good. I now allow the pure substance of Your Love to move in and through me.

My heart swells in gratitude as Your prospering power fills all aspects of my life.

You are continually blessing me with the wealth of vibrant health, material sustenance, joy-filled activities, and loving community.

You bestow upon me the riches of fulfilling work, inspired ideas, harmonious relationships, assured faith, and deep peace.

Through the power of Christ within, I pray and exclaim, "Thank You, God!" Amen.

Elizabeth C. Dixon

My Source

In the sacred sanctuary of my soul, I grow in the awareness that You, God, are the Source of All that Is, and therefore the Source of all my Good.

My very being exists in Your Perfect Love. Vital Divine Energy courses through my body, my mind, my spirit, and my environment.

Your vision of me is one of wholeness, plenty, well-being, and authentic happiness.

Your Love springs forth in me and from me as joy, creativity, and animation. From You the good desires of my heart are made manifest in my life.

I behold All that You constantly demonstrate in thanksgiving and gratitude!

Thank You, God! Amen.

Complete Good

O God, Source of All That Is, You have placed me in this bountiful universe with access to everything I would ever need or want to thrive and experience fulfillment and joy in living.

In my unlimited imagination I envision an abundance of coming blessings. In Truth, All that I can conceive of is already mine. As I purposely transport my feelings and emotions into the place of having already received, tangible demonstrations in this plane are activated. I revel in my Good. My spirit swells in gratitude and in celebration.

As I practice the Power of co-creation that You generously share with me, my experience of living is transformed. I realize that there is nothing I cannot be, do, or have. You are my Partner in all my endeavors—I cannot fail!

May my thoughts stay fixed on You, God, the All Good. In You I am always complete.

My expectation is fulfilled! Thank You God! Amen.

Winnowing

Holy Spirit, breathe across me and blow away the chaff of negative thoughts and emotions that clutters my mind. May doubt, fear, and criticism be swept away, like mere particles of dust and detritus, by the welcome breeze of Your Presence so that they cannot affix in my consciousness.

Let the wholesome kernels of confidence, faith, love, and kindness remain and prevail, germinating within to give me renewed vigor and enthusiasm for living.

Remind me, Gentle Spirit, that I create my reality and my perceptions by way of the thoughts I choose to sow and nurture. You have given me a marvelous fertile imagination that I use constructively and lovingly.

In inspired partnership with You, I think and live positively, generously, and on purpose, and my life becomes a rich harvest of blessings. My cup is pressed down, shaken together, and overflowing! Thank You, God! Amen.

Clarity

Taking time apart in prayer, I step away from mental turmoil, indecision, confusion, and doubt by going within to my sacred center. How pleasant it is to detach from cares and worries and bask in the tranquil Constance of Spirit.

Here, in communion with The Most High, I encounter Your supernatural wisdom and instruction.

Whisper gently to me, O God, Your Counsel. It may be revealed gradually as an image that slowly comes into focus, or it may burst upon me as a flash of inspired insight.

I wait here in easy expectancy for Your Guidance. I will realize I have intuited Your authentic inspiration when calm spreads throughout my being and I feel deep peace.

Then I will know with confident assurance what is mine to do. Thank You, God! Amen.

Sacred Decision

What a wondrous and powerful gift You have given us, O God, by granting us free will!

In every moment I am at the place of decision. In every instant I am choosing my thoughts, my words, and my actions. Even my perception of self and my vision for the world are choices.

In You I have immediate access to all the resources I need to make the best decisions for the Highest Good for myself and everyone affected.

The guidance I seek comes from within, from that Sanctuary of stillness and peace where I meet You.

As my awareness of Your Presence expands, I am conscious of Divine Direction coming forward.

I welcome Your Guidance and know that by following It in faith and with confidence, I move with grace through every situation and circumstance.

I will know each decision is in alignment with You as I experience deep peace in its wake.

Choice by choice I co-create my life and my world with You, O Loving, Creating God!

Through the Power of the Christ within, it is so! Amen.

V

Liberation of Forgiveness

Willing to Forgive

I have come to realize, Gentle Spirit, that forgiving is not condoning or excusing—it is releasing the hold a past event, action, or person has on me. Forgiveness releases me from the pain of the past. This pain no longer serves me. Refusing to forgive is a decision to continue to suffer.

I have the power, by Your example and with Your loving assistance, to forgive and end my suffering. I am willing to make the decision to forgive. I deserve freedom. I deserve serenity.

When I let go of grievances of the past, I experience instant deliverance and deep peace. Imagining, I take a moment right now and notice how wonderful it feels in my heart space, mind, and body when I release and enjoy liberation and peace.

You have shown us, Lord, that forgiveness is the most powerful healer of all. I am ready to be healed; I am willing to forgive. Forgiveness is Your sacred water that cleanses my soul. I am willing to forgive.

I now fully realize that forgiveness is the surest way for me to undo mental and emotional suffering and pain, to be truly healed and happy! Even my body relaxes and releases toxic residue as I begin to truly forgive.

I no longer withhold my love from anyone. I no longer withhold love from myself. As I no longer see myself as a victim, it becomes easier and easier to forgive.

As I forgive, I feel unburdened, lighter, and in closer affinity with You, O God!

In the Name of Jesus Christ who teaches us to forgive, I forgive. I am free! Amen.

Elizabeth C. Dixon

Gift to Myself

Gracious Spirit, You are continuously kind and patient with me; show me how to be kind to myself.

Whatever has transpired before is now in the past, and I have learned to do and be different and better.

I am willing to stop nurturing guilt with accusatory thoughts. I am willing to give all remaining feelings of blame, regret, and anguish over to You, God.

Sharing sacred space with You, I become more compassionate for the part of myself that has felt injured or troubled.

In Your Presence my center regains its equilibrium. As a kindness to myself, I give my burden over to you, God.

I am at my core a loving and merciful person. Let me now extend that love and mercy that is my Christ nature to myself.

I treat myself with gentleness and tenderness. Henceforth I go easy on myself, knowing Your Love supports me.

As I allow love and compassion for myself to grow, I begin to realize a new and welcome feeling coming forward: a willingness to forgive myself as You have already forgiven me. In grace and generosity of spirit, I now forgive myself.

I am at peace—I am healed! Thank You, God! Amen.

Pure Heart

Create in me a pure heart, Lord!

I invite You to wash away all residue and traces of judgment, suspicion, resentment, anger, blame, malice, deceit, pride, regret, and shame.

As I surrender into Your cleansing Love, I am refreshed and restored to wholeness, virtue, and joy. Why would I resist Your promise of new life? I submit to You now.

May I now extend authentic forgiveness and compassion toward my sisters and brothers, remembering that You already have given me unconditional, eternal love and complete forgiveness despite my own errant thoughts and ways.

May Your Sacred Heart be the model of my innermost being.

I am renewed! Praise God!

Be kind to one another, tender-hearted,
forgiving each other, just as God in Christ
also has forgiven you.
Ephesians 4:32

VI

Sacred Space for Another

I Pray With You

I am holding sacred space with you my sister. I am keeping the high watch with you, my brother. Know that in Spirit we are one and you are never alone.

I behold the Christ in you; I salute the divinity within you that is your core Essence. My vision of you is of wholeness and plenty. I see you vibrant with life, infused with peace, and aligned with your Good.

Recognize now the perfect pattern of the Christ that abides within you. Know that you are the child of Almighty God, heir to the Kingdom of All Good and Perfect Love.

Within you is the transcendent God-potential that is greater than circumstances, larger than outer appearances. Yours is a spirit of Power, and Love, and Self-discipline!

I affirm and declare free-flowing God Consciousness moving in and through you now.

Embrace the Truth of your Being and claim your Good in expectation and thanksgiving. Through the unfailing Christ Presence, so it is! Amen.

My Loved One

O God, You know my heart and the concern I am carrying for my loved one. I affirm that she whose name I now speak and lift up before You is Your beloved Child, precious in Your sight.

I am comforted knowing that even in this very moment, You, God, are moving in and through her, quickening within her, bringing her increased health and prosperity, greater confidence and strength, Divine order and protection, and deep peace and joy to her experience of living.

You have promised us, Lord, that we shall decree a thing and it shall be established. I am filled with gratitude, knowing that she is now wrapped in the comfort and support of Your Perfect Love.

May she recognize Your Light shining upon her path and Your Presence in all aspects and activities of her life.

In the Name and by the Power of the Indwelling Christ, it is so. Thank you, God! Amen.

Your Beloved

As I bring this Your Beloved to You in prayer, God, I affirm that the Light of Your Perfect Love is ever shining upon him.

May he be filled with the peace of knowing that Your Love transcends all appearances and understanding.

May he be assured that Your Love is now transforming every fiber of his being— renewing his mind, lifting his heart, and invigorating his body.

May he open himself to Your continuous Presence in his life, and may he witness in awe and delight as You transform every activity and circumstance he encounters into Divine order for his highest good.

May he realize the birth of the Christ Light within him every day as he allows It to fill his whole being and shine through him as love, forgiveness, healing, peace, and joy.

Thank you, God, for the gift of the Christ, abiding in us as you continually renew and sustain us. Amen.

Creature Cara

Gentle Spirit, receive this beloved animal companion into your care and keeping.

Restore her to energetic wholeness and vitality in her new form of being.

Bless him in his ongoing with peace and contentment.

May any lingering memories she might have of trauma, pain, or fear dissolve into nothingness.

Let her bask in our continuing heart-felt love. May she sense our nearness and support as she proceeds into this next stage of existence, free and filled with renewed vigor.

Let our memories of him dwell on our happy times together when he delighted in the prime of his life, exulting in the sheer joy of living.

Thank you for the gift of sharing his life and love with us.

She has been one of our most cherished blessings as a member of our family. Comfort us as we grieve her physical absence.

Strengthen our faith, we pray, that in You, nothing is ever lost, and our beloved (*name of pet*) is safe and thriving just on the other side of the veil.

Indulge us in our hope that he is reunited with friends and loving companions who now welcome him into their midst.

Fill us with assurance that we will have a loving reunion when we ourselves are ready to cross over into the realm of the non-physical, with her and in the tender company of every animal and person we have ever loved.

We thank you for our beloved (*name of pet*). Amen.

Make Peace

O God! Let not my heart be troubled; neither let me be afraid!

Only the Peace that God gives can heal the world. I believe and affirm God's Peace is now transforming this erring world, beyond my understanding.

In the stillness of prayer, I envision God's Peace enfolding our world leaders. I affirm guidance, strength, integrity, wisdom, and clarity for each of them, and I extend my prayer blessings of love and peace.

God's Love is my compass as I pray for all people across the planet, affirming harmony and goodwill throughout the Earth. God's Peace spans the continents, uniting us as one human family.

I envision a world at peace as I give thanks for God's healing Light and Love. Let there be Peace. It begins with me!

And it is so! Amen.

Peace I leave with you; my peace I give to you;
not as the world gives do I give to you.
Let not your hearts be troubled,
neither let them be afraid.
John 14:27

VII

Transitions through Eternity

My Companion in Grief

O God! O God! In this despair I can barely breathe—now breathe in me; breathe for me.

I invite you into the depths of my grief. You know the desolation of my heart and the reeling of my mind.

Be here with me now as my silent Witness.

Hold me. Beat my heart for me. Carry me from this moment into the next moment.

Only in You do I continue to exist. You never leave me.

Little by little I begin to become aware of Your Presence.

I can feel the warmth and strength of Your Perfect Love now wrapping around me.

Your Holy Presence is a soothing balm that comforts my soul.

Just as You are here intimately with me, so you are also with my loved one, for You are Omnipresent.

I am open and ready to receive Your assurance that beyond the veil that limits my present understanding, All Is Well!

In the name of the Christ, it is so! Amen.

Repose

As I turn within and sense the Presence of Your Spirit, God, I feel assured in the depths of my being that my true essence is non-physical; I am not this body vessel.

I am coming to realize that Your Plan and Timing for me may indeed be physical healing—or—it may be my transition into a new experience of existing that is beyond my current understanding.

Surely, Your Energy is all around me, ready to do Its perfect work in me . . . as I allow . . . as I trust . . . as I align seamlessly with You by releasing and surrendering.

Your Grace is perfect, everywhere present, at all times. Therefore, in Truth, I am always whole, beyond diminishment or dissolution of the physical.

Any suffering I experience is in my resistance! My peace does not come through my will, through my control; it comes by releasing my perceived self into the expansion that is the Great I Am.

As I relinquish the illusion of control, I am free.

As I allow my awareness to merge into the Whole, I experience blessed relief and deep peace.

In faith I now surrender into Your all-encompassing Love. Your Love is eternal.

Your Love enfolds me, and All Is Well.

I continue in the I Am. It is so! Amen.

Eternal Life

There is no death—You have assured us! Yet, in fear we have given power to the illusion. We allow this dark idea to haunt our thoughts and feelings and dominate us with dread.

Your Beloved Son, our Brother, Jesus Christ, has already demonstrated victory over mortality and vanquished the delusion of oblivion. Indeed, He has assured us that He goes before us to prepare a Place for us!

I believe, Lord—help Thou my unbelief! Help me to witness Your myriad Signs and Synchronicities that prove our perpetual ongoing in the Light of Your Love.

What God has created can never be undone. We are living Eternal Life now!

God is my Glory! Amen.

Let not your heart be troubled: you believe in God; believe also in me. In my Father's house are many mansions: if it were not so, I would have told you. I go to prepare a place for you. And if I go and prepare a place for you, I will come again, and receive you unto myself; that where I am, there you may be also. And where I go you know, and the way you know.

John 14: 1-4

VIII

Incarnation & Ascension

Divinity Incarnate

As we celebrate Your gift of Jesus in this Holy season, may Christ be born anew in me, on Christmas Day and every day. May Your Perfect Love find in my heart a welcoming manger.

May I witness in awe and delight as Christ Light fills my whole being and shines forth through me as hope, peace, joy, and love.

As I realize and embrace the Christ within, I am transformed! In Christ I evince Your Divine Plan for mankind individualized. May Christ express through me and bless the world!

Thank You, Lord, for the gift of Your Son, our Wayshower, our Master Teacher, our Elder Brother—our Savior who leads us back to You! Emmanuel has come! I rejoice! Amen.

Christ in Me

Loving, Creating God, in this sacred moment my awareness of Your Presence now expands. I begin to realize that, indeed, You abide in me!

You are active in me and through me and around me. You are my constant and instant Source of peace, provision, and abundant Life. The Christ of my being is One with You!

The Resurrection is Your promise to us all, personally and universally, that in Your Love and Light we overcome the limitations of the temporal world and experience victory over darkness and death.

I have immediate access within to Your restorative Power! One with God and All That God Is, I am reborn anew, again and again, filled with vitality and joy.

In Christ I ascend! Alleluia!

Elizabeth C. Dixon

Easter Reverie

In this season of rebirth, and always, Spirit makes all things new. As the sap rises in the pith of the tree warmed by the spring sun, the dynamic creative Essence of God quickens in me.

I now allow God's vitalizing flow of Life Force Energy to move through me, as me. As the Christ rises within me, I am a new creation! Christ in me—my hope of Glory!

As my awareness of God's Living Presence in and around me expands, my life, my activities, and my relationships unfold in new ways, immersed in Light and Love.

He *breathes* in me—I am reborn! Hallelujah!

Therefore, if anyone is in Christ,
he is a new creation;
old things have passed away;
behold, all things have become new.
2 Corinthians 5:17

IX

Celebration in Gratitude

Be Gratitude

O God, Source of All, I thank You that there is always *something* to be grateful for—I can always find a blessing that fills me with gladness when I am willing to notice!

Indeed, I often experience the lifting and shifting that happens within me when I open my awareness of the bounty and beauty all around me . . . when I recognize Your provision and grace at work in my life.

Yet, what if the purest gratitude is a spiritual state of being that requires no reason—no trade-off—to simply be?

I can imagine myself in a state of appreciation that is not transactional, not dependent on my perceiving or receiving.

I am ready to experience a state of genuine gratitude that is above and beyond the consequence of my having received, beyond reason.

Gentle Spirit, cultivate in me a quality of gladness and appreciation that transcends outward circumstances and appearances. May I exist and proceed through my life in a state of gratitude that is unconditional and free-flowing from deep within me.

As I exude gratitude, I align with The Most High and I am blessed and a blessing. In this wondrous state of being, I experience life joyously: I AM Gratitude. The Christ of my being declares it to be so! Amen.

Elizabeth C. Dixon

A Child Arrives

In awe and wonder I peer into the face of this precious newborn and see God expressing in human form.

Fresh from the ethereal Realm, she has arrived in original innocence, a miracle of creation, unique and never to be repeated in all the Universe.

Lord, you have honored us with a sacred charge—the care and nurture of this eternal soul on her sojourn into this temporal setting.

You have entrusted us with her life and growth, and we embrace this cherished gift in amazement and gratitude. Our lives are immeasurably enriched and blessed by her presence in our family.

May we ever be mindful that she is Your beloved child, intrinsically valuable and worthy, deserving of our richest provision of love, devotion, sustenance, protection, guidance, and constancy.

We look to you Lord, for Your inspiration and encouragement and wisdom as we walk the path of life together, knowing you are the Light on our way, and we are Yours.

We treasure her! Thank You, Creator God! Amen.

Elizabeth C. Dixon

Splendor

I behold the magnificence and grandeur of Your Creation in awe, O God!

Incarnate in human form in this tangible plane, I am able to experience this world as a physical creature—subject to the natural, physical laws of this dimension.

Through the enlivened senses of this physical body temple, I can joyfully perceive the opulent demonstrations that Your Word manifests upon this spatial earthly realm.

I delight in the grand spectacle as light refracts and reflects, sound resonates and echoes, and energy moves mass and matter to clash, integrate, destroy, and recreate.

Sensing, feeling, moving, resting, touching, savoring, making, exploring, seeking, finding, holding, intoning, caressing, satiating—the myriad and varied gifts of human being and doing.

I am both observer and participant in this ever-expanding spiral dance of becoming.

What a dynamic stage You have placed me upon in which to develop my sentience and evolve my consciousness!

I marvel at Your Ways, O God—Yours is the Glory! Amen.

X

Master, Teach Us to Pray

Source that Is All, Your Name is Sacred.

You fill us with the Truth of Your Perfect Love and Light.

Your Intention becomes our activity—in manifestation as in Divine Mind.

Sustain us continually with Your Transcendent Substance.

And loose us from the entanglements of our mistakes, as we have released others from their offenses.

Help us resist the seduction of false appearances, and deliver us from delusion, stagnation, fear, and death.

For You are the One, the Truth, and the Life Eternal. Amen.

Prayers for New Thought Christians

Submitted for your consideration, I present my interpretation of the prayer taught by Jesus to his disciples when they asked him how to pray, based on the original Aramaic and subsequent Greek texts, as well as mystical and metaphysical Christian tradition.

Elizabeth C. Dixon, Author

Elizabeth C. Dixon

Duodenaria Prayer Process

*An Affirmative, Incremental
Prayer Process over Twelve Days*

Form your intention and mentally place it at the center of this sacred activity.

Slowly read each Day's Prayer numerous times throughout the day, both silently and aloud.

Contemplate each Prayer's deepest mystical meanings, sentence by sentence, allowing the words to become the words of your own heart.

End Day 12 by reading all the Prayers in sequence.*

Rejoice and give thanks for Blessings received and Blessings forthcoming.

For expanded spiritual practice, recite The Lord's Prayer—Master, Teach Us to Pray—before each of the Duodenaria Daily Prayers.

As a brief intensive, the process can be condensed to twelve hours.

Day 1—Invoke

O God, here I am—fully revealed in Your Presence.

You know my heart. You know my need.

You know my fears. You know my sense of helplessness.

You know my mind's turmoil.

I turn now to You, my Source and my Comfort.

Only in You can I find resolution and peace.

You hear my prayer; Your Answer is already coming! Thank you, God!

Amen.

Day 2—Surrender

Lord, I submit now to You.

As I relax my resistance, I dissolve into the warmth of Your Light.

As I allow Your Love to wash over and through me, I am soothed and centered.

I rely fully on Your Omnipotence to order chaos and to silence noise, both within and without.

How mysterious are Your Ways—it is by surrendering to You that I am freed!

And so it is.

Amen.

Day 3—Release

Creator God, I willingly give up any errant notion of my power or control over others and outcomes. I let go.

Help me also to loosen my grip on the thoughts and beliefs that are causing me confusion and pain.

Whatever troubles are still distressing me, I now give to You.

As You lift my burdens from me, I feel immediate relief and renewed hope.

I gratefully relinquish all my cares and concerns to Your perfect provision.

All is well.

Amen.

Day 4—Entreat

You, O God, are Source; All That Is has its inception in You.

You know the longing of my soul even before I form the words to ask for Divine assistance and intervention.

My heart's desire is safe in Your keeping. You shelter my fragile faith and increase it as I draw closer to You.

You are already actively bringing about fulfillment for my highest good and for everyone concerned.

I leave my request with You in sacred trust, believing Your promise that as I ask, I shall receive. Thank you, God!

Amen.

Day 5—Atone

My honest and contrite appraisal reveals that along my way I have countless times mis-stepped or missed the mark.

I feel the sting of remorse and regret sufficiently to own my culpability and to resolve to do better.

I am now willing to do and be different; please help me, Lord.

Even in my flawed state, I am able to glimpse Your grandeur, and I am in awe. Your purity and peace compel me to come closer to You.

Though I have erred and strayed, You enfold me in Your unearned grace and have already washed me with Your forgiving Love.

In humility and gratitude, I accept Your cleansing absolution. I am free!

Amen.

Day 6—Forgive

In my growing awareness of Your intimate nearness, Master, I am coming to realize that now is the time for me to unburden myself of stored hurts and resentments.

Harboring pain, anger, and animosity creates a bitterness deep within that seeps into every aspect of my life, spoiling my wellbeing and robbing me of authentic joy.

I now turn any lingering wounds and contempt I have let fester over to You, God. Your purifying Light cleanses my soul. The balm of Your sanctifying Love restores me to wholeness.

In the place of injury, I now nurture a spirit of genuine mercy and forgiveness. I generously extend love and forgiveness to others and to myself.

My spirit is expanded, and my heart is lifted! Thank you, God! Amen.

Day 7—Trust

In You alone I place my faith and trust, O God. I willingly suspend my reliance on temporal appearances and my own limited human understanding.

You are the Assurance my heart hopes for.

I step out onto the invisible substance of Your provision, believing—yes, indeed knowing—that Your Omnipotence is at work and in charge everywhere and always.

I submit to Your perfect timing. Poised and patient, I await the perfect fulfillment of Your promises in anticipation and gladness.

I commend myself to You, Lord of my being.

Amen.

Day 8— Receive

Open me up as an aperture, O God, and flood Your Love Light into the dim recesses of my heart and mind!

Now receptive and expectant, I allow Your Presence and Power to move in and through me.

I am filled with elation as Divine Possibility expands in me.

Already I sense the mystery of transformation occurring at deep levels within—I am becoming a new creation in Christ!

Oh, the Wonder!

Amen.

Day 9—Listen

In Spirit and in Truth, I am never alone. When I become still and enter the Silence within, Your voice whispers inspiration and counsel to me, God.

May I feel the companionship of Your Presence wherever I go. Day by day, may I heed the quiet urging of sublime ideas You generate within me. Let me notice the inner nudging of Supernatural instruction.

You graciously surround me with loving unseen agents in the forms of angels, saints, spiritual companions, guides, and friends. I welcome their assistance and support as I discover Your answers unfolding as manifestations in my life.

I never walk alone—Your guidance is ever within and around me. In Your care and keeping I live in confidence and gratitude!

Amen.

Day 10—Peace

As I become still and fully present in this moment, I turn my focus within and feel You drawing me into Your Peace, O God.

Immersed in Your Love and Constancy in this inner sanctuary, I am soothed and calmed. One with You, peace infuses my being.

No outer circumstance can disturb the serenity of my soul. Your Peace abides in me and sustains me always.

The peace You impart is the promise that All is well and Good is unlimited. I radiate tranquility, grace, and confidence as I engage with life.

The Christ Light of Peace is my assurance and strength. It is so!

Amen.

Day 11—Synchronicity

Your Ways are elegant and enigmatic, Lord. You order the movement of the stars and the sequence of the seasons. The timing and details of all events are directed by Your Hand.

You harmonize every circumstance and element of our lives—beyond appearances or our understanding. In Love and in Truth, You make all things work together for our ultimate Good.

My soul's sacred progression of becoming evolves as a dynamic spiral within the Whole. May I nurture a consciousness that aligns with the flow of Your Perfect Plan. I embrace possibility with an inner aspect of allowing and glad anticipation.

May I discern Holy signs and synchronicities along my way and be assured of Your exquisite coordination and influence ever present in my life. Your Will and Intention for each of us are beneficent and loving. We are Yours!

Thank You, God! Amen.

Day 12—Gratitude

Amazed and delighted, I behold the wonder of Your creation, O God!

My mind and heart expand in gratitude and awe! Creator and Source of all that is, Your love endures forever!

You bless me beyond measure. You are the very life energy that thrills in and through me. I am one with You, inseparable, merged with the Whole of All, complete.

Your Perfect Love enfolds everything and everyone, constantly and forever.

Awaken in us the knowing of Your Supreme Spirit now moving in our midst, establishing Divine order and Holy resolution.

Thank You for Your mercy and grace; thank You for Your guidance and provision; thank You for Your healing and protection. Thank You for Your peace.

We go forth as confident co-creators with the Most High, mighty to do what is ours to do.

We live and move and have our being in You, O God, and all is well.

In the Name and by the Power of Christ Being, I affirm and declare these Truths to be so!

Amen.

Every good gift and every perfect gift
is from above, and comes down from
the Father of lights, with whom
there is no variation or shadow of turning.
James 1:17

Additional Resources

Books on New Thought Prayer

Butterworth, Eric
    The Universe is Calling: Opening to the
Divine Through Prayer

Hasbrouck, Hypatia
    Handbook of Positive Prayer

Foulks, Frances W.
    Effectual Prayer

Fox, Emmet
    The Golden Key

Holmes, Ernest
    Prayer: How to Pray Effectively from
The Science of Mind

Suggested Reading

If you would like to learn more about New Thought/Metaphysical Christianity and wish to understand the concepts better, below is a Suggested Reading List that is a starting point, but it is by no means exhaustive.

New Thought (also Higher Thought) is an American spiritual movement with roots in Classical Metaphysics, Transcendentalism, and Deism that coalesced in the 19th Century. The movement was launched in large part by the writings and lectures of Phineas Quimby and Emma Curtis Hopkins.

Central to New Thought are practices of mind power, positive thinking, affirmations and denials, affirmative prayer, co-creating with God, the law of attraction, creative visualization, spiritual healing treatments, and prosperity principles.

Some of the well-known churches and spiritual organizations that had their inception in the New Thought Movement are:

Elizabeth C. Dixon

Religious Science (Science of Mind), Divine Science, Jewish Science, Christian Science, Unity, Centers for Spiritual Living, International New Thought Alliance, and Christian libertarianism (as epitomized by Dr. Norman Vincent Peale).

Listed in order of original publication dates; newer editions are available.

Emma Curtis Hopkins
　　　High Mysticism, 1888
　　　Scientific Christian Mental Practice, 1888

H. Emilie Cady
　　　Lessons in Truth, A Course of Twelve Lessons in Practical Christianity, 1896

Ernest Holmes
　　　The Science of Mind, 1926
　　　A New Design for Living, 1959

Prayers for New Thought Christians

Charles Fillmore
    Talks on Truth, 1922
    The Twelve Powers of Man, 1930

Emmet Fox
    The Sermon on the Mount, 1938

Eric Butterworth
    Discover the Power Within You, 1968

Ervin Seale
    Take Off from Within, 1971

Rev. Paul Hasselbeck, et. al., Unity Institute, 2007
    Metaphysics I An Overview of the Fundamental Teachings of Unity
    Metaphysics II Practical Application of the Fundamental Teachings of Unity

About the Author

Elizabeth C. Dixon, MA, CHt, is a writer and editor of spiritual and personal development non-fiction. A life-long inquirer and student of metaphysics, she served for over ten years in the Prayer Ministry of Unity Church of Jacksonville, Florida, generating prayer letters and creating Prayer Chaplain curricula. For four of those years, she served as a trained, active Prayer Chaplain, praying with Congregants and leading Prayer Services and classes.

She is also a practicing Hypnotist trained and certified by the International Medical and Dental Hypnotherapy Association. She is mother of two adult daughters and grandmother of six grandangels. Elizabeth lives with her husband Charles and their big chocolate Labrador Retriever on the shore of the Intracoastal Waterway in Jacksonville, Florida.

An Invitation

If you enjoyed this book and found inspiration and insight herein, I'd be very grateful if you'd give the book a 5-Star rating and post a short review on Amazon.

Your support truly makes a difference and I personally read each and every review.

Simply go to: Little Book of Prayers for New Thought Christians on Amazon.

You may also follow me on Facebook and Goodreads.

Little Book of Prayers for New Thought Christians on Facebook

GoodReads Author Elizabeth C. Dixon

Thank you for your interest, engagement, and sharing this book with others. Be Blessed!

Elizabeth C. Dixon

Made in the USA
Middletown, DE
30 January 2022

60099531R00070